Freddy Adu

By Jeff Savage

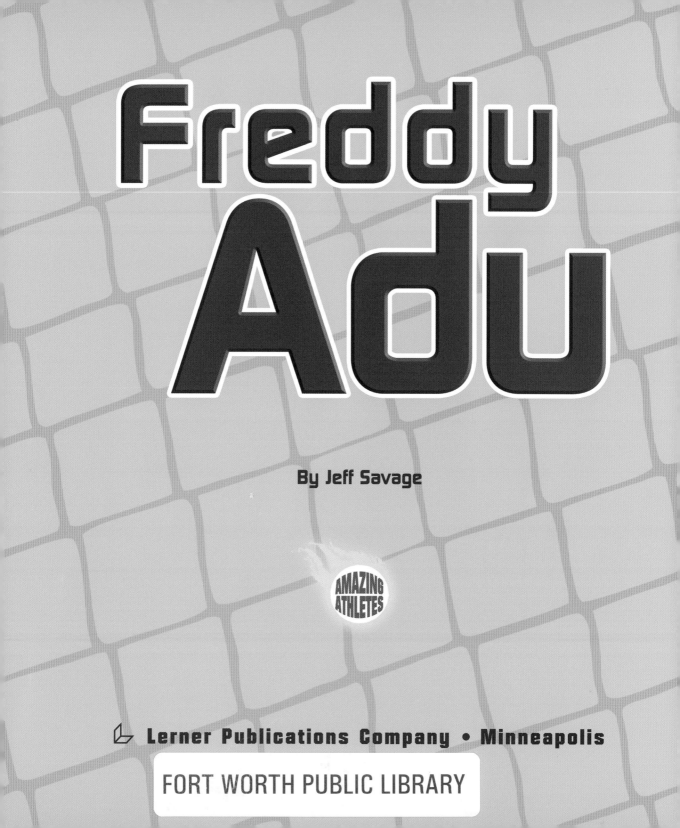

AMAZING ATHLETES

Lerner Publications Company • Minneapolis

Lerner Publications Company
A division of Lerner Publishing Group
241 First Avenue North
Minneapolis, MN 55401 U.S.A.

Website address: www.lernerbooks.com

Library of Congress Cataloging-in-Publication Data

Savage, Jeff, 1961–
  Freddy Adu / by Jeff Savage.
      p.   cm.—(Amazing athletes)
    Includes index.
    ISBN-13: 978–0–8225–3430–3 (lib. bdg. : alk. paper)
    ISBN-10: 0–8225–3430–4 (lib. bdg. : alk. paper)
    1. Adu, Freddy, 1989– —Juvenile literature. 2. Soccer players—United States—Biography—
Juvenile literature. I. Title. II. Series.
  GV942.7.A34S28 2006
  796.334'092—dc22   2005019323

Manufactured in the United States of America
1 2 3 4 5 6 – DP – 11 10 09 08 07 06

TABLE OF CONTENTS

Freddy *(center)* watches from the bench as his team plays.

STARTING EARLY

Freddy Adu was nervous. He squirmed on the bench. He peeked into the stands to see hundreds of fans wearing his black D.C. United soccer jersey. "Fre-DEE! Fre-DEE!" the fans yelled. They had filled RFK Stadium in

Washington, D.C., to see Freddy play. The 2004 **Major League Soccer (MLS)** game between the San Jose Earthquakes and D.C. United was nearly half over.

Why was everyone so excited? Freddy was just a boy. He was 14 years old. He was about to become the youngest athlete in professional team sports in more than 100 years. Freddy was already the most famous player in the nine-year history of MLS. And he hadn't even played in a game!

Two young fans hold up a sign for Freddy at his first game.

ARE YOU READY FOR SOME FREDDY?

Freddy jokes around with Coach Nowak during a practice in Washington, D.C.

Freddy did not **start** the game against San Jose. D.C. United coach Peter Nowak did not want to put too much pressure on him. Finally, in the 61st minute of the game, the coach called for Freddy. The fans erupted with cheers as Freddy ran onto the field. Horns blared.

In Freddy's first season in 2004, attendance for D.C. United games was nearly double the average for other MLS games.

Confetti swirled in the air. High up in the stands, Freddy's mother, Emelia, was jumping up and down and clapping. "Maybe he's nervous," she said. "I know I am."

Freddy heads onto the field during a game in his first season.

Freddy was just five feet seven inches tall and weighed 140 pounds. He was the smallest player on the field. D.C. United forward Dema Kovalenko kicked the ball to Freddy. Freddy kept the ball glued to his foot as he moved past a **defender**. Then he passed it ahead to a teammate. The crowd roared. As the game wore on, Freddy got several more **touches**. Most times, he quickly passed the ball. A few times, he flashed the ball-handling skills that make him great.

D.C. United won the game, 2–1. Freddy walked with his teammates past the cheering crowd to the locker room. Butterflies still danced inside his stomach. "I'm glad it's over," he said. But for Freddy, this was just the beginning.

Freddy was born in Ghana, Africa, in the port town of Tema.

COMING TO AMERICA

Fredua Koranteng Adu was born June 2, 1989, to Emelia and Maxwell Adu. Freddy grew up in the western African country of Ghana. His family lived in a fishing port called Tema. It is a custom in Ghana to give sons the same name, so Freddy's younger brother is also named Freddy. Freddy's younger brother goes by the nickname Fro.

Freddy was two when he received a package from his uncle in the United States. It was a soccer ball. "His eyes lit up," said his mother.

Freddy spent hours a day outside kicking the ball against a wall. More than once, he kicked the ball too hard and broke a neighbor's window. Freddy's mother had to buy a new window. By the age of four, Freddy was playing barefoot on dirt streets. He usually played against boys much bigger and older than he was. "They taught me to be tough," said Freddy.

Freddy likes many American foods. But he also loves dishes popular in Ghana. His favorites are goat meat with okra (a kind of vegetable) and an African stew called jollof rice.

Freddy attended The Heights School in Potomac, Maryland.

When Freddy was eight, his family moved to the United States. They settled in a one-bedroom apartment in Potomac, Maryland. But the family's new life in the United States wasn't easy. Freddy's father left the family. Emelia had to work two full-time jobs to earn enough money to support her sons.

Freddy leaps up to head the ball during a game played in 2003.

DAZZLING MOVES

Freddy was a bright student. He even skipped the third grade! But he did not know how to play organized soccer.

At school one day, a fourth-grade classmate spotted Freddy dribbling the ball with his feet. The boy invited Freddy to play in a game with his team. Freddy showed up on the field wearing black jeans, an orange sweatshirt, and a Mickey Mouse hat. He looked nothing like a soccer player. But when the action started, Freddy dazzled everyone. Left foot, right foot—pop-pop-pop—he juggled the ball as if he were dancing.

Freddy is good at many things. He scored 28 points in his first school basketball game at the age of 10. In his first art contest, as a fifth grader, he won the county's top prize.

Freddy juggles the ball.

Freddy practices his soccer skills. He plays near his family's townhome in Potomac in 2001.

After the game, the coach of the other team went to Freddy's house. His name was Arnold Tarzy, and he invited Freddy to join his team. Even more, he opened his home to the Adus. Freddy and his brother often stayed overnight at the coach's house. Freddy still calls him Uncle. Soon after meeting Coach Tarzy, Freddy was playing for an Under-14 Boys team called the Potomac Cougars.

When Freddy was 10, he traveled to play in a **tournament** in Italy. Everyone expected the United States team to lose badly. Instead, Freddy led his team to the championship and was named Most Valuable Player. An Italian team was amazed by Freddy's skills. They were so impressed they wanted Freddy on their team. They offered Freddy a **contract.**

The man on the left plays for Inter Milan, the Italian team that offered Freddy a contract.

The team would pay Freddy to join their **farm system.** Freddy's mother could hardly believe it.

Still, she said no. Italy was too far away. Other soccer clubs in Europe offered Freddy rich contracts. The money was tempting. But Freddy's mother wanted him to stay in school.

At the age of 13, Freddy had already been playing with the U.S. Under-17 Men's National Team for a year.

GOING PRO

Freddy was 12 when his mother allowed him to leave home. In 2002, he joined the U.S. Soccer Federation's development program in Bradenton, Florida. He was the youngest player on the U.S. Under-17 Men's National Team. Freddy spent most of his time doing two things—studying and playing soccer. "It was hard being away from home," Freddy said, "but it was worth it."

Freddy plays against athletes that are usually much bigger than he is.

Coach Trevor Moawad helped Freddy learn how to use his skills when playing against the bigger, older players. He worked hard and improved his game. Even though he was younger than most of his teammates, he soon became the best player on his team. Over the next two years, Freddy scored a team-best 57 goals in 87 games. In one game against Sierra Leone, he scored the key goal. It helped the United States qualify for the FIFA World Youth Championship tournament.

By the time Freddy was 14 years old, he was about to finish high school. He was eager to play professional soccer. Freddy began lifting weights to gain strength.

In January 2004, Freddy was the first player chosen in the MLS **draft.** Some people wondered if such a young kid could make it in a professional league. But Freddy wasn't worried. "If you're good enough, you're old enough," he said, flashing his dazzling smile.

Freddy doesn't let it bother him that he is the youngest player in the MLS.

Freddy poses for a picture with his mother, Emelia, after he signed a contract with D.C. United.

Freddy signed a contract to play for D.C. United. He would make $500,000 per year for four years. This was twice as much as any other player in the league earned. "The first thing I'm going to do is build my mom a gigantic house," said Freddy.

Sporting equipment company Nike signed Freddy to a $1 million **endorsement** deal.

Freddy began appearing on such TV shows as *60 Minutes* and MTV's *Total Request Live*. He got to meet superstars like basketball's Shaquille O'Neal. His favorite moment came when he got to star in a commercial with Pelé, the greatest soccer player ever.

Pelé is the only professional soccer player to score more than 1,000 goals.

Freddy's family lives in a big five-bedroom house in Rockville, Maryland. The basement is a recreation room. It has a pool table and wall of speakers for music. "That's the coolest part," says Freddy. "I can hang out with my friends, play pool, listen to music and dance."

Everyone was impressed with Freddy. Sometimes the attention was too much. "When it started, it was the coolest thing in the world, 'cause that's what every kid wants—you want to be famous," said Freddy. "But after a while you're just like, 'Please, leave me alone!'"

Fans hold up signs that spell out Freddy's name at a D.C. United game in 2004.

REACHING THE BIG TIME

The Freddy Adu craze swept through the 2004 soccer season. Street vendors sold Freddy T-shirts and buttons. Fans held up signs and banners with his picture. On the field, Freddy played **forward** and **midfielder** with spunk. He swerved and slashed through defenders. He threaded passes through tiny openings. Sometimes he got knocked to the ground. But he always got back in the action.

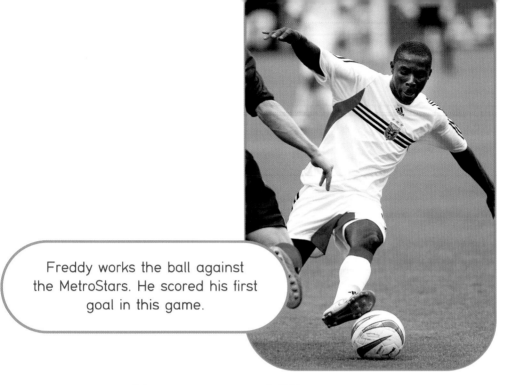

Freddy works the ball against the MetroStars. He scored his first goal in this game.

Freddy scored his first goal as a pro against the New York/New Jersey MetroStars in April. He sneaked behind two defenders and sent a crossing pass into the goal with his left foot. A month later, he dribbled past three Los Angeles defenders and blasted a rocket high into the net. Freddy finished the season with five goals—third-most on the team. D.C. United rolled through the playoffs and beat the Kansas City Wizards to win the MLS Cup 2004 title.

D.C. United was strong again in 2005, with Freddy leading the way. "He's done things that have blown some minds," said teammate Ben Olsen.

When Freddy was not playing in MLS, he played for the United States in tournaments. In one match at the 2005 FIFA World Youth Championship tournament in the Netherlands, he scored the winning goal. In another, he made an **assist** on the game-winning goal to win the group title.

Freddy knows to stay positive when things do not go his way. "I'm not always going to have the greatest game of my life," says Freddy. "There are going to be games when I absolutely stink. That happens to everybody. So it will be up to me to regroup and try to find a way to bounce back."

Freddy displays his footwork at the 2004 MLS All-Star game at RFK Stadium.

Watching Freddy play, it is easy to forget that he is just a kid. He likes to eat Snickers bars and Lucky Charms cereal, play video games on his PlayStation2, and hang out at the mall with his friends. But soccer always comes first. "When I'm on the soccer field, I'm at my happiest," says Freddy. "When I'm out there, I'm not scared of anyone. I just want to play and have fun."

Freddy trains hard but still has fun playing soccer.

Selected Career Highlights

2005   Became the youngest player to be named MLS
         Player of the Week
         Led the United States to FIFA World Youth Championship
         group title

2004   Scored his first MLS goal against New York/New Jersey
         MetroStars
         Became youngest American in over 100 years to play
         for a professional sports team
         Signed richest contract in MLS history
         Named to MLS All-Star team

2003   Scored four goals to help the United States advance to
         quarterfinals in FIFA World Youth Championship
         tournament
         Led U.S. Under-17 Men's National Team in goals

2002   Was youngest member of U.S. Under-17 Men's National Team
         Finished second in goals on U.S. Under-17 Men's National Team

Glossary

assist: a pass to a teammate that helps that teammate score a goal

contract: a written deal signed by a player and his or her team

defender: a soccer player whose job is to stop the other team from scoring

draft: a yearly event in which teams pick new players

endorsement: a deal in which a player receives money to promote a company's products

farm system: a series of teams of different skill levels on which players train

forward: a soccer player whose main job is to score

Major League Soccer (MLS): the top professional league of men's soccer in the United States

midfielder: a soccer player whose main jobs are to pass the ball and defend

start: to play when the game starts

touches: when players make contact with the ball

tournament: a set of games held to decide the best team

Further Reading & Websites

Murcia, Rebecca Thatcher. *Freddy Adu*. Hockessin, DE: Mitchell Lane Publishers, 2005.

Freddy Adu: The Soccer Phenomenon
http://www.freddyadu.com
Freddy's official website features news, statistics, trivia, photos, and a diary from Freddy.

The Official Website of D.C. United
http://dcunited.mlsnet.com
The D.C. United website includes the team roster and schedule, late-breaking news, biographies of past and present players and coaches, and much more.

The Official Website of Major League Soccer
http://www.mlsnet.com
MLS's official website provides fans with the latest scores and game schedules, as well as profiles of players and coaches and soccer training tips.

Soccer America Magazine
http://www.socceramerica.com
The popular magazine available in print and online features the latest news and information about the world of soccer.

Sports Illustrated for Kids
http://www.sikids.com
The *Sports Illustrated for Kids* website covers all sports, including soccer.

Index

Photo Acknowledgments

Photographs are used with the permission of: © Robert Laberge/Getty Images, p. 4; © George Tiedemann/NewSport/CORBIS, p. 5; © Jason Reed/Reuters/CORBIS, pp. 6, 21; © Doug Pensinger/Getty Images, p. 7; © Rob Tringali/SportsChrome, pp. 8, 25; © Jak Kilby, p. 10; Potomac Almanac, pp. 12, 16; © Eric Miller/Getty Images, p. 14; © David Kadlubowski/CORBIS, pp. 15, 29; © Reuters/CORBIS, p. 17; © Gary Bogdon/NewSport/CORBIS, p. 19; © Suhaib Salem/Reuters/CORBIS, p. 20; © STAN HONDA/AFP/Getty Images, p. 22; © Bettmann/CORBIS, p. 23; © AP/Wide World Photos, pp. 26, 30; © Hyungwon Kang/Reuters/CORBIS, p. 28.

Cover image: © David Kadlubowski/CORBIS